Her Majesty's Inspectorate

Aspects of Primary Education

THE
EDUCATION
OF
CHILDREN
UNDER
FIVE

London: HMSO

Contents

PREFACE

This publication, the first of a series of inspection reviews of primary education, reports and comments upon recent trends and issues which have influenced the education of children under five.

The publication exemplifies good practice and gives particular attention to the curriculum for young children and the implications for this of the introduction of the National Curriculum.

We hope that the publication will be of interest and helpful to those who are responsible for the organisation and teaching in schools, to teacher trainers and those concerned with providing for the under-fives both within and outside the maintained sector.

INTRODUCTION

1 Maintained educational provision for children under five includes nursery schools, designated nursery classes and units, and classes with under-fives admitted early to primary school. Education for the under-fives is also provided in combined nursery or family centres, often jointly funded by local education authorities (LEAs) and social service departments (SSDs).

2 Some 45 per cent of under-fives receive education in nursery and primary school classes but the variation between LEAs is considerable, from over 80 per cent in some to less than 20 per cent in others. The overall figures for Greater London, the metropolitan districts and the county authorities are 49 per cent, 64 per cent and 36 per cent respectively; there are considerable variations within as well as between these groups of authorities.*

3 Of the under-fives receiving education in maintained provision approximately 24 per cent are in nursery schools or designated nursery classes and units, while 21 per cent are admitted early to primary school. Most of those admitted early to school are four years old. Some authorities have traditionally admitted children early but as rolls have fallen and space has become available this practice has become more widespread, and most now admit children before they reach statutory school age. The most common practice is to admit children at the beginning of the school year in which they are five. The latest statistics show that as many as 62 per cent of four-year-olds are in infant classes. Some are in reception classes alongside older children within the same year group; others are taught with children aged five and six years and, sometimes, with seven-year-olds.

4 HMI regularly assess the work of children under five across the range of educational provision described above. With the agreement of SSDs we have also assessed the educational components of some combined nursery or family centres.*

5 This document is based upon the inspection of the work of children under five undertaken in the period 1985–88. It includes full inspections of nursery and primary schools and an illustrative sample of work from some 300 visits made by early-years specialists across the full range of maintained educational provision in England. The findings from these inspections raise a number of important issues affecting the education of children under five.

6 The quality of education for children under five is greatly influenced by the type of provision within which it takes place. Taking all factors into account, children under five in nursery schools and classes generally receive a broader, better balanced education than those in primary classes. The work is well planned with a suitable emphasis on purposeful play and exploratory activity. Other conditions associated with the more frequent occurrence of better quality education in nursery schools and classes include: a narrower age band of children; better adult/child ratios; accommodation which in the main is purpose-built, or well adapted to the age group; better material resources; and more teachers experienced in teaching three- and four-year-old children.

7 In a small number of primary classes activities are well planned for the under-fives, oral work is excellent and the interaction between adults and children is enhanced by the effective participation of parents. In most such classes, however, the education of children under five, though sometimes given a high priority, often suffers from a lack of breadth and balance so that the curriculum is not as well matched to their educational needs as it should be. For example, there is often insufficient exploratory and practical work to support the children's developing understanding of ideas

*DES Statistical Bulletin 7/89. *Pupils Under Five Years in Each Local Education Authority in England.* January 1988.

*HMI Report *Combined Provision for Under-Fives: The Contribution of Education.* DES, 1988.

5

and language before they start out on the formal work more appropriate to later stages of learning.

8 There are signs of improvements, however. The growing number of under-fives entering primary classes has heightened the schools' awareness of the needs of this age group and there is recent evidence of better practice, usually where early-years advisers and the teachers have focused attention upon four-year-olds in school. As a result, in some primary classes, accommodation, the curriculum and methodology have been suitably adapted to the needs of the four-year-olds. Good curricular guidelines and effective in-service education have helped some teachers to improve the provision and the teaching for children under five. The greatest benefits have accrued where LEAs have provided sufficient teachers and other adult staff who are suitably trained and experienced in working with this age group, and where resources are sufficient in quantity and of suitable quality. In such cases most of the authorities concerned allocate the same financial allowances to four-year-olds admitted early to school as they do to infant-aged children generally; they sometimes provide additional grants for provision of extra equipment.

9 The quality of education for the under-fives in some LEAs suffers from a shortage of appropriately trained teachers and advisers with expertise covering this age group of children. Many authorities have had to appoint teachers whose training and experience have not equipped them to work effectively with the under-fives. Not surprisingly such teachers find it difficult to provide and teach a suitable curriculum for young children. They need effective guidance and training to work successfully with this age group. The designation, under the LEA training grant scheme, of in-service training for teachers working with four-year-olds in primary classes will go some way towards providing this support.

10 Teaching young children, like all teaching, demands a high level of organising ability and skill; a good understanding of what is to be taught and of child development; a wide repertoire of teaching and learning styles; and an appropriate range of materials and resources. If new teachers of young children are to understand what constitutes appropriate provision for the under-fives and how it relates to the early years of compulsory schooling, it is important that their initial training covers at least the age range of three to seven years to enable them to contribute as a member of a primary school team.

PLANNING THE CURRICULUM: SOME PRINCIPLES UNDERLYING THE EDUCATION OF CHILDREN UNDER FIVE

11 Children joining a nursery or primary class for the first time have already made major steps in learning. Through the things they do and talk about with their children, parents play a crucial part in that early learning and will continue to be a strong influence on the young child's development. An important aspect of the role of the teacher is therefore to explain to the parents what the school is seeking to achieve and so help them to extend their children's learning. A successful partnership between the home and the school enables parents to understand how they can best contribute to their children's education; an early appreciation of their role in these respects is often vital to securing parental support throughout a child's schooling. But the teachers also benefit from sharing the parents' greater knowledge of the child as an individual and from learning something of the child's home background.

12 Many but not all teachers welcome and value parental help in the classroom, though it makes new demands on their management and communication skills (1)*. Working with children alongside teachers also helps some parents to

become aware of the new relationships which their children form as they settle into school (2). In every case, however, such

*Figures in brackets refer to photographs.

2

arrangements should be planned within the framework of aims and objectives for the work as a whole and evaluated accordingly.

13 For most children starting school, whether in a nursery or primary class, brings them into contact with their peers in greater numbers and for longer periods than they have previously experienced. They also have to adjust to being away from their parents for longer than most have experienced before. Consequently, ensuring that young children feel secure in their new circumstances and quickly learn to co-operate and respond positively to others (3) are important objectives for teachers of young children to bear in mind when planning the

3

curriculum. They must be especially sensitive to the need to ensure a smooth transition from home to school.

14 Children start school with different levels of confidence and competence. Some have had a broad range of experiences and can relate well to others, speak clearly, draw, count and read. At the other extreme, some children, for whatever reasons, have not begun to develop such competencies and are still heavily dependent on others, behaving at times almost like babies. Teachers have to take account of this range of needs when they plan the curriculum for young children and ensure that the work is suitably differentiated.

15   A broad and balanced curriculum for the under-fives places emphasis upon the major aspects of children's physical, emotional, social and cognitive development. In whatever setting, high-quality education is characterised by:

i. extending the children's range of profitable learning and experience beyond that which can easily be provided within the family but in ways which are complementary to it;

ii. using a range of materials and equipment in planned and progressive ways, which stimulates and advances the children's social, emotional, physical and cognitive development;

iii. teaching which stimulates and builds upon children's curiosity; enables them to learn through planned worthwhile play activities; encourages them to experiment; to explore their environment; to be imaginative and creative; to plan, implement and reflect upon their experiences;

iv. developing children's early knowledge, understanding and skills in ways which provide a sound basis for later education, for example the ability to listen and to talk about and record their experiences with increasing understanding, competence, confidence and fluency.

16   Purposeful play features strongly in good pre-school education. It is not a free and wholly unstructured activity. Through the selection of materials and equipment, and the combination of these (4), teachers ensure that, in their play, children

encounter the learning experiences that they intend. By their involvement, comment and questions, teachers, nursery nurses and other adults help children to learn from such activity. Play that is well planned and pleasur-

able helps children to think, to increase their understanding and to improve their language competence. It allows children to be creative, to explore and investigate materials, to experiment and to draw and test their conclusions. Teachers know that such experience is important in catching and sustaining children's interests and motivating their learning as individuals and in co-operation with others.

17   Because so much of the work in the early years is practical and built around activities, and because the pattern of children's learning favours a good deal of choice and change in activities throughout the school day, there is always a danger of the programme becoming fragmented and disparate. Adults can find themselves coping with the management of resources and the movement of children at the expense of

teaching effectively. Good planning, which includes the involvement and deployment of the members of staff and any voluntary helpers, is of crucial importance if these problems are to be avoided.

18 Teachers and other adults who work with the under-fives are in a good position to plan activities jointly and to implement and review the curriculum so that it is coherent and progressive for each child. The interdependence of the different adult roles favours joint planning and, in most cases, the school's size is also a significant factor in establishing efficient networks of communication, making it possible to respond quickly if changes in the programme are necessary. In the best circumstances, the teaching is informed by a careful assessment of the overall programme and the response of each child to the learning activities which are provided. Judgements about the children's learning are recorded so that their progress can be planned and monitored over time.

19 Certain general principles that inform the planning and evaluation of the curriculum for children of compulsory school age hold true for the under-fives. As for older pupils, the curriculum for young children needs to be broad, balanced, differentiated and relevant; to take into account the assessment of children's progress; to promote equal opportunities irrespective of gender, ethnic grouping or socio-economic background; and to respond effectively to children's special educational needs.* The Education Reform Act (ERA) calls for a balanced and broadly based curriculum which:

i. promotes the spiritual, moral, cultural, mental and physical development of pupils at the school and of society; and

ii. prepares such pupils for the opportunities, responsibilities and experiences of adult life.†

These aims are relevant also to the curriculum for the under-fives.

20 The nine areas of learning and experience discussed in *The Curriculum from 5 to 16: Curriculum Matters 2* * are widely recognised as essential for all children including the under-fives. They provide a helpful framework for the planning and analysis of the curriculum for young children. These areas are the aesthetic and creative, the human and social, the linguistic and literary, the mathematical, the moral, the physical, the scientific, the spiritual and the technological. Within and across this framework the knowledge, understanding, skills and attitudes essential to the work with the under-fives may be developed concurrently. Increasingly, in planning the curriculum for these children, teachers use this framework though they often find it helpful to combine the areas of learning and experience in a variety of ways.

---

*Young children with Special Educational Needs. An HMI Survey of educational arrangements in 61 nurseries. DES, 1983.
†Education Reform Act 1988. Part I Chapter I(2).

*The Curriculum from 5 to 16: Curriculum Matters 2. HMSO, 1985.

ILLUSTRATIONS OF GOOD PRACTICE

21 The illustrations of classroom practice which follow show how aspects of some of these key areas of learning and experience can be combined and implemented. They also exemplify the important principles below that underpin the effective teaching of children under five:

i. while young children learn effectively through self-motivated and planned educational play and the practical activity associated with it, there are many other

5

equally valuable ways of learning, for example, listening to stories (5), music, the teacher or other adults relating their own experiences or explaining and exploring phenomena and other ideas in discussion;

ii. much effective practice involves the children in activities which relate to several aspects of learning at any one time;

iii. thorough planning and an assessment of the children's progress through the close observation and recording of their individual responses to the provision are features of effective practice.

22 High-quality planning that acknowledged the children's own interests underpinned the success of a range of work with the under-fives in an inner city school in the north of England. The school has a nursery class and also admits four-year-olds to the reception class. The work for all the children under five is planned jointly at times when both full- and part-time members of the teaching and ancillary staff can contribute. Work on the theme of 'coverings' was planned to encompass several areas of learning, and to extend the children's early mathematical, linguistic, physical and social skills and their abilities to observe and compare similarities and differences:

The four-year-olds in the reception class studied clothing, fruit, animals' coats and the outside surfaces of objects. The teacher read a story, 'Mr Bear's Shipwreck', in which some of the characters drank the milk from a coconut. The teacher brought a coconut into school, and the children looked at it, discussed the attributes of the shell, helped to break it open and tasted the milk and the flesh. Two of them made coconut macaroons in the home corner assisted by a member of staff. The connection between the whole and the shredded coconut used in the macaroons had been discussed earlier; texture and taste were compared; the recipe was selected from a book; and the processes of weighing, mixing and washing up were successfully completed by the children. In association with a Caribbean Festival in the area other fruits were investigated. After hearing the percussion instruments used at the festival some of the children also made shakers. They each used two yoghurt pots which were fastened together after the children had selected and put in lentils, peas, sesame seeds or black-eye beans as 'sound-makers'. Subsequently the shakers were covered, using glued paper strips. By the questions she asked the teacher encouraged the children to make mathematical comparisons and to think about how to cover the curved and flat surfaces, to estimate the area and select the most appropriate size of paper strip to complete the task:

'Do you think that piece is long enough? Will it go right round the shaker?'

'Which part of the shaker will that piece of paper go around, the middle or the top? Is it too short for the widest part of the shaker?'

Anna rattled her shaker and Joseph asked what was inside it. At first Anna pointed to the black-eye beans. She easily recalled the name when her teacher reminded her of the earlier discussion about the black eye being similar to the pupil in her own eye. Joseph was disappointed that his shaker no longer created as much sound since it had been covered with papier-mâché. In order to help him to discriminate between sounds the teacher encouraged him to think about the contrasts:

'How is it different, Joseph? Is it a softer sound? Why do you think it is not so loud and clear?'

Other children tried out and compared the shakers, to decide if they also sounded different when they were covered with paper. Joseph danced around, first using his shaker and then clapping his hands to create a rhythm. The impact of his discovery and his ability to make links with previous experience was clear later in the day when he was putting on his outdoor clothes. He clapped his hands and remarked, 'My claps are not as loud with gloves because my hands are covered up.'

In the school's nursery class work on the theme of 'wheels' was stimulated by an attractive display of wheels from different vehicles, together with a collection of artefacts including two old sewing machines. The children's paintings showed careful observation and the written question 'Can you think of something with wheels?' resulted in an interesting list of objects named by the children. Three children constructed vehicles from waste materials. The teacher encouraged them to select the most suitable materials for their constructions and to think about the concept of width:

'Perhaps you could find a very narrow box; here is a thin box; do you think that one might be too thin?'

The domestic play area had been converted and resourced to provide opportunities for making imaginary journeys and for using small wheeled toys. A four-year-old girl, Jane, was sitting inside a large wooden box with a semi-circular brick in her hands, silently 'driving her car'. The teacher helped Jane to relate the concepts of time and distance.

Teacher: 'Have you far to go?'
Child: 'No not very.'
Teacher: 'How long will it take to get there?'
Child: 'Four minutes.'

As Jane continued playing in the car, Akim arrived and climbed in beside her. He looked at the brick steering-wheel and then hurried off, returning with a real steering-wheel from the display. The two children sat for some time companionably 'driving' together until they were interrupted by three boys who tried to get in the car but Jane told them calmly, 'We've not got there yet.' This was accepted and the boys turned to the nearby collection of toy vehicles and started to play with them, driving complicated routes around each other and making comments about the qualities of their individual vehicles.

23 With young children, many productive ideas are generated through play and practical activity. The quality of the discussion and the adults' questioning at the time, and later, are important in enabling the children to consolidate and increase their knowledge and understanding of important early mathematical, aesthetic, linguistic and scientific concepts. In these activities the children also acquire considerable social skills: interacting within a group, and learning about sharing and fairness in taking turns.

PERSONAL, HUMAN AND SOCIAL LEARNING AND EXPERIENCE

24 It is widely recognised that children's self-esteem is profoundly influenced by the regard in which they are held by others. The quality and consistency of relationships in all aspects of school life are important in shaping children's regard for themselves and others. Young children, like others, take time to develop new relationships, particularly with those they may at first see as different from themselves. Good social relationships are often fostered by planning a curriculum which provides opportunities for the children to learn more about the lives and work of the people in school and in the wider community (6). The

6

children's awareness of diversity in custom and culture and their respect for and understanding of cultural differences are effectively developed through planned activities and the use of carefully selected stories and picture-books, artefacts and materials.

An infant school with a nursery class providing for an ethnically mixed community in the north-west

As part of a multi-cultural project funded by an educational support grant (ESG), the nursery assistant discussed with the children their distinctive features and facial characteristics as a preparation for painting self-portraits. The children spent a long time mixing colours from dry powder paints seeking for the shade which best matched their skin colour. This was a well handled session which dealt with ethnic difference with great sensitivity and allowed the children considerable autonomy.

Care was taken to match the work to the different levels of understanding and competence in the group; a child experiencing the new sensation of pushing his finger into paint was encouraged to talk about it and to use his fingers to apply the colour to paper; techniques for mixing colours and using different kinds of brushes were discussed with the more experienced children. Once completed, the portrait paintings were carefully mounted and displayed in the classroom.

25 As the work proceeds, teachers are increasingly concerned to help young children begin to develop important attitudes, for example, a sense of fairness, justice, honesty, truthfulness and care and respect for each other and for living things (7). Group discussions and role play are often well used to help young children to come to terms with emotions such as joy and sadness, fear and dislike. Much effective work also draws upon the children's experiences at

7

home, sometimes to help them adjust to events which they have not understood or have found upsetting. In these ways teachers establish sound attitudes and good patterns of behaviour.

26 Young children are naturally interested in their homes and the local community. The work people do provides many valuable starting-points for learning about the interdependence of human communities and the contribution of individuals to the common good. Given appropriate resources, doctors, nurses (8), postmen and firemen are some of the roles which children often choose to adopt in their play.

8

These experiences provide the foundation for drama at subsequent stages.

Four-year-old children in a large first school in the south. This work was prompted by an extended in-service course for teachers focused on the National Writing Project

Imaginative hospital play was developed in a variety of ways and had a strong association with the early stages of writing. Additional resources had been provided to turn the home play area into a hospital. The 'kitchen' had become a small servery for the production of drinks and snacks. Along with some toy surgical equipment a range of different uniforms for 'doctors' and 'nurses' and 'ancillary staff' had been provided.

Activities to support the hospital play included looking at carefully chosen books about doctors and hospitals, discussing the roles and activities of the various professionals and exchanging experiences about the children's own visits to the doctor or the hospital. Adults took part in the play to increase the children's understanding of hospital procedures, to provide and enlarge vocabulary and to give information about the use of various materials and items of equipment. The high quality of the play reflected the careful provision of resources and supporting activities and information. 'Parents' with their 'children' first checked in at the reception desk where details of their family background, names and nature of illness were written down by the 'receptionist'. These notes were given to the doctors who began examining the children, suggesting a 'diagnosis', then undertaking a 'remedy'. The adults maintained the children's interest by providing additional items such as tweezers and cotton wool or by suggesting possible courses of action to be taken. For example, it was suggested that before amputating a child's leg perhaps his parents should be told! This led to the use of the reception desk telephone to contact parents and the news was then broken to them. At various intervals 'ancillary nursing staff' provided meals and snacks for the staff and patients.

27 Children's understanding of the present and its relationship to the past is developed through recollecting and sequencing events that have taken place during the day, week or year or by discussing developments from babyhood, sometimes using the children's own photographs. Their awareness of change is fostered through work about the neighbourhood and the domestic and everyday lives of their families. Grandparents and others sometimes share their knowledge about changes in population, buildings, roads or street furniture. The collection, observation, handling and discussion of related artefacts often extends such learning, which is the basis of later historical understanding. Schools generally focus upon broadly based themes or centres of interest to plan such work.

A nursery class in a small primary school in an inner-city area in the north-west

The work in the nursery class is planned around carefully selected themes based on the immediate environment and embracing wide human and social experience. Work on 'holes and tunnels' involved a visit to the railway station. The children became very interested in the network of tunnels and subways. The staff provided a collection of pictures, books and artefacts. Using a variety of media some

9

10

of the children drew and painted pictures of things seen during the visit (9, 10). The children and adults assembled displays of hollow, round and cylindrical objects. One group of children worked at the sand tray creating an intricate network of tunnels using wet sand. Other children organised a variety of 'tunnel' activities in the outdoor area. They constructed a network of tunnels using gymnastic apparatus including barrels, a collapsible plastic tunnel and a variety of large cardboard boxes. The teacher provided torches which extended and enriched the range of activity. The construction activity

offered rich opportunities for solving technical problems and developing language and mathematical ideas.

In the half term following their work on the 'holes and tunnels', the children began to think about 'change' related to 'moving house'. To make the work as realistic as possible it was decided to move the home corner from one of the classrooms to another. Together the children and the teacher discussed how this should be done before setting about the task.

The dolls were prepared for the journey and placed in the baby buggy. Materials and equipment were sorted into kitchen and bedroom items and packed into appropriately labelled boxes. One child reminded the others that they might want a cup of tea when they arrived, so the kettle was put on the top of the kitchen box. The boxes were then moved to the new site. Inside the 'new house' the group decided that a staircase was needed; stage blocks were used for this purpose. After some discussion about the location of the staircase it was placed in one corner. Logistical problems had to be solved such as where pieces of furniture should go; whether the main furniture should go in before the boxes with the small equipment; how to get the sink units in a line because the new house was a different shape; where people would sit; and which area was to be the bedroom.

28 This activity involved the children in a considerable amount of planning, organising, sequencing of events and problem-solving. The two adults participated by prompting some children, drawing others in, keeping the momentum going and making suggestions which set off new lines of thought and enquiry. They were careful to involve all the children and encouraged the sharing of gender roles (11).

11

29 Successful work ensures that the intellectual demands upon the children increase in step with their growing competencies and introduce skills and ideas needed in later more demanding activity.

A nursery school in the south Midlands serving a socially mixed catchment area

As part of the theme 'Around and About', the children went walking in the locality. Photographs were taken of buildings in the area as well as of the children standing at their own front doors. These were used to make a simple board game devised by one group of children. The game showed the children's routes to school, drawn by the children, and passing well known landmarks

13

12

represented by the photographs (12). The children's figures, cut out from the photographs, were used to represent the players. The children had also drawn plans and pictures showing streets, shops and other features which interested them (13). The teacher used a printed plan of the locality to extend the children's mapping skills. They made a model of a street and constructed houses from corrugated cardboard and waste materials.

In their imaginative play other children focused on aspects of a building site which had interested them; they wore safety helmets and made their own constructions using large wooden bricks and planks (14).

Others worked at a tray with wet sand using trucks, a bulldozer, ramps and spades. Associated with this work was an excellent display of charcoal and pencil sketches made on the site visit, supplemented by photographs borrowed from a local estate agent. A range of drawing materials such as pencils of different thicknesses and colours, charcoal, pens, chalks, pastels and crayons were available so that children could choose how to represent their impressions of the visits.

Talking to informed adults and looking at books, photographs and small-scale maps increased the children's understanding of place and locality, which was developed by the use, in the children's play and exploratory activity, of constructional kits, natural materials, playmats, model railway lines and road networks to make imaginary layouts and three-dimensional models of the neighbourhood. Thus the conventional classroom materials and the local environment supported the children's learning about aspects of human and social development.

14

30 Listening, speaking, reading and writing are fundamentally important activities in young children's learning. Good provision promotes ideas and responses from the children which they may communicate in a variety of ways but the modes of language claim special attention. The quality of adult language which the children encounter and their opportunities to talk with adults about their work are important to their progress. Many children of three and four already use language flexibly and for a variety of purposes. Good early-years education encourages them to extend and use these skills. Their vocabulary, the complexity of their speech and their confidence are developed as an integral part of their activities when they discuss and express points of view, recall the past, speculate about the future, and describe clearly places, events, situations, and their feelings.

31 In talking about their experiences young children frequently reveal a remarkable competence in offering information, comment and questions, some of which lead to framing hypotheses. Conjecture and deduction are well within the capabilities of young children when, for example, everyday phenomena are observed.

A nursery school in a London borough

A group of six children worked in the outdoor area with their teacher. They had found a snail on a bush and explained in detail how they had gone looking for worms but had noticed holes in the leaves and found the snail. They assumed that the snail had made the holes and must have eaten the leaves. Since it had retreated into its shell, the children speculated about how it would eat and where its mouth was. There was some interesting discussion and speculation about how the snail got up to the top of the bush where it was found, since it had no legs. They watched the snail emerge from its shell and move across the leaf. The children decided to keep the snail in a box in the classroom for a day or two and to watch it, using a magnifying lens.

32 As children's oral competence develops they can be brought to see the relationship between speaking, listening and the written word. Children are well used to seeing print in the home, in the streets, in the supermarket and in a variety of other places they visit with their parents. Many of them already have an interest in reading, some are readers already, and teachers of young children seek to sustain and develop this skill at a pace appropriate to each child. Others need to learn about beginning

15

at the front of a book, reading from left to right, that there is a sequence to the story, that pictures contain information but that the print is read. Teachers ensure that such children learn how to handle, enjoy and obtain information from picture- and story-books, and so begin to build the early stages of teaching reading on a basis of interest and familiarity with reading material of quality (15).

A nursery school in the south-west

One boy brought a book about the seashore to the nursery. He was very interested and enthusiastic about it. Although he could not read the text, with three friends and an adult he looked at the pictures for some time. The children asked questions and made deductions and comparisons.

'If we put all our legs together we would have more legs than a crab.'

They observed the pictures very carefully indeed. They looked at a picture of a sea urchin – one child said that its spikes looked like a horse-chestnut. The next picture was of a cuttlefish and the adult asked them the difference between a cuttlefish and a crab. This led to talk about bones and skeletons and the children felt their bones and began to discuss how they were different from the crab and the cuttlefish. Throughout, the adult read snippets of the text so that the children began to understand that the print contained interesting information beyond what they could deduce from the illustrations.

33 In many classrooms the children's interest in reading is similarly fostered through such early experiences of print and books (16).

16

A nursery school in the south-west

Two girls aged three and four were sharing a nursery rhyme book, open at the rhyme 'Peter, Peter, Pumpkin Eater'.

> Child 1: 'I know that one, shall I read it to you?'
> Child 2: 'Yes' (snuggling up close to her older friend).
> Child 1: 'There was a mother and a dad and they lived in a pumpkin and then went to Tim's house.'

She closed the book and picked up another. She looked carefully at pictures and then turned to the front of the book. With her arm around the younger child, she began to tell the story.

> Child 1: 'She waved goodbye to her mummy, she went to sleep but she woke up again and there was a knock on the door and it was the milkman, no, the postman.'
> Child 2: 'No the cleaner.'
> Child 1: 'No it is the milkman.'

She continued reading in a deep voice,

> 'Bring the milk in.'

She then pointed to a picture.

> 'That's not the mother because she's got white shoes and a pigtail.'

She then continued with the story.

> 'They sat down and had a chat. Look, there's the window cleaner cleaning all the windows. But where is the mummy? She's coming in a minute. Shall we read it again?'

> Child 2: 'No, but it's nice isn't it?'

34 Effective teachers know that when children have reached the important stage of being able to recall stories and use books in this way, they are often ready to relate meaning to the printed word more accurately and the teachers help them to do so. Teachers also begin to teach children about the relationship between letters and the initial sounds of words in the stories they read and hear; children are often fascinated by this and soon offer suggestions of other words that begin with the same sound. Most quickly learn to read and write their own names (17)

17

and to label familiar objects. Such experiences provide good opportunities for teachers to bring the early stages of reading and writing together so that learning in the one activity strengthens learning in the other.

35 There is much interesting practice that takes account of the need for a secure and enjoyable foundation for listening and speaking, reading and writing in classes with children under five. On the way to literacy children are introduced to poetry and prose of increasing range and complexity. Traditionally stories and rhymes take their place alongside modern literature. The materials chosen frequently reflect the culturally diverse nature of our society by drawing upon stories and tales from a range of cultures. At this early stage too, much can be done through the careful selection of stories to help children to see that the interest and capabilities of girls and of boys are of equal importance.

36 Sometimes nurseries and schools have collections of good-quality picture-books which parents can borrow to read to their children at home. Many schools help parents to know more about those picture story-books which will best promote talk, exploration and a healthy appetite for reading. Useful links are often established with local public libraries which the children visit, either with teachers or with parents.

37 Alongside the initial stages of reading, children often record their ideas, experiences and feelings through drawing, painting and writing. Teachers encourage children to write as part of their play activities by providing writing materials for them to record, initially in their own invented symbols, such things as shopping lists and telephone messages. Areas of the classroom are sometimes set up as offices or writing centres (18), and as the children become eager to write and their symbols closer to accepted letter forms, they are taught, usually individually, to form letters and print in conventional

18

ways. To extend their interest in writing teachers often record what the children say about their experiences (19), sometimes in individual or class booklets, or as labels to accompany their paintings and models or classroom displays.

19

A nursery school in the south

The imaginative play area had been organised to provide a hairdresser's shop with improvised hairdryers, a sunbed and a table with shampoos, combs, brushes, hair clips and wigs (20). In the shop's reception area there was a desk with a telephone, an appointment book and appointment cards. Throughout the day the children used this area regularly and the telephone booking and appointment book entries were a centre of particular interest. The appointment book showed clearly the children's emerging writing skills. Written messages contained recognisable letters as well as invented symbols. Much of the interest was related to the exciting variety of writing materials available. The appointment book and cards offered good opportunities for teachers to discuss with the children the appointments which were made as well as their precise timings. Later in the day a parent helper sat in the area and worked with the children on activities such as manicuring, hair combing and drying and, again, the appointments book served as an important focus for discussion.

38 This work exemplifies the benefits of well planned provision and effective adult interaction. The children were encouraged to reflect on their own experiences and to order and sequence their thinking. The incidence of child-initiated conversation was high and showed that the children were developing oral competence, a fundamental prerequisite to early literacy. Writing was closely related to the activity advantageously and adults, including parents, were able to participate easily to support the work.

20

39 Successful schools ensure that the children engage in many activities which develop their mathematical understanding. Direct experience, for example of handling materials and making constructions, inevitably increases children's understanding of ideas about order, difference and quantity. Their ability to use mathematical language discriminatingly and accurately is increased through well planned practical activities and play experiences designed to

that at every stage they talk with children about their activities so that their understanding and skills are extended.

40 Children learn to sort, match and order during domestic play, or when setting their places for lunch (23), as well as when they use mathematical equipment such as sets of objects that are different (24), for example, in size, shape and colour.

21

22

2

24

help them understand aspects of number, weight, size, capacity, time (21) and measurement. Such experience includes sorting and comparing, and encourages children to think about relationships such as 'heavier' and 'lighter', 'smaller' and 'larger', and to know about shapes (22). Effective teachers ensure

These are important experiences that help children to understand one-to-one correspondence and subsequently the process of counting. They begin to appreciate ideas of scale through the use of miniature road and rail tracks and vehicles alongside the larger ones they construct from bricks and boxes.

Through effective teaching and the use of suitable equipment with sand and water young children begin to understand capacity, conservation and comparative measurement. Enjoyable and worthwhile activities such as playing games and singing number songs and rhymes help children to begin to see sequences and patterns in number, and encourage their interest in mathematics.

41 In the best circumstances the children's recording of number activities is based upon their secure understanding of the counting process and their ability to match number symbols with a group of objects. This is often acquired through structured activities.

A nursery class in a primary school in London

The teacher had provided a variety of well selected games. Three children and an adult played a dice game in which the children had to pick up a card showing the same number of spots as the dice. For two of the children this involved much careful counting, but the third, a four-year-old, immediately recognised the numbers. She scored 3, 3, 3 and said, 'I've got three threes, that's . . . nine.' During the next round she dropped the dice. 'That's nothing', she laughed, 'and nothing makes no difference.'

In the last two rounds she scored a 2 and a 1. The teacher asked if she knew how many spots she had collected. 'Well, a two and a one make mmmm three . . . four threes, that's . . . twelve.'

Then she carefully counted all the spots to confirm her calculations.

Through the routine of playing a co-operative game the children had learned several important mathematical and social skills in an enjoyable context. The use of well-chosen but simple apparatus allowed the more able child both to consolidate early learning and to develop more complex ideas.

42 Through effective planning, observation and well-timed intervention teachers extend the children's ability to use language accurately to express ideas of shape and size.

Four-year-olds in an infant school in a large city in the south-west

The teacher placed on the carpet a piece of patterned material folded so that it took the shape of a trapezium. The children suggested names for it: a boat, a sail, a pirate's hat. Through skilful questioning some of the vocabulary of position – 'opposite', 'between' – was introduced. The material was unfolded to make a larger (triangular) shape which two children were able to name correctly. Most were able to identify the shortest and longest sides and to distinguish the shorter and longer of any two of the sides. The teacher generated anticipation through the folding and unfolding of the material, maintaining the children's interest throughout.

43 Children are often encouraged to think about mathematical ideas, such as similarity and difference, in activities concerned with scientific, technological or physical skills.

A nursery unit in a primary school in the home counties

The children chose wood for model-making from a box which contained pieces of varying shape, size and thickness. They discussed with the adult which nails were to be used to join pieces of wood together. The lengths of different nails were carefully compared with the thicknesses of the wood. One child selected a piece of wood and rejected it as he estimated it was too thick to be joined to another piece using the nails available. He then chose a thinner piece of wood. The work offered many opportunities for estimation and problem-solving in the course of making simple constructions.

44 Children also have opportunities to solve mathematical problems and to develop spatial awareness when they use constructional equipment such as bricks and other building materials (25, 26).

25

26

A nursery school in London

A group of three boys worked co-operatively with bricks in constructional play. One boy took a selection of small rectangular and triangular bricks. Using early ideas of tessellation he arranged and rotated them so they would form a rectangle. He added some curved pieces and then decided it would be a road.

> Child 1: 'There mustn't be any gaps or the cars will fall off.'
> Child 2: 'How can they get off the road?'
> Child 1: 'I'll find a sloping piece for a ramp.'

They then attempted to build a bridge but initially placed the pieces so that they caused an obstruction in the road. The first boy rearranged them, constructing ramps and supports to take the bridge over the road.

Having discovered that ramps needed to be provided for a bridge, he applied his ideas to each of the structures he had made, eventually testing the completed track with a car and making the adjustments he felt necessary.

45 In these examples, the adults used classroom resources or the immediate environment, and the structured and spontaneous events that each provides, to best advantage. Sometimes teachers represent mathematical ideas for children, for example, by means of models, figures and pictorial representation as part of classroom displays (27, 28). Given such stimulus, some children begin to experiment with their own forms of recording, primarily by using objects or drawing; some are able to use and understand number symbols and are encouraged to extend their skill and understanding. Successful work takes account of the mathematical skills, ideas and knowledge that children need to learn in order to benefit from the later stages of education, and teachers plan accordingly. Thorough planning and preparation also help teachers to use teaching time effectively, for example, for working with groups and individual children to make the best of differentiated work.

27

28

SCIENTIFIC LEARNING AND EXPERIENCE

46 There is considerable congruence between the national objectives for the 5–16 age range* and the nature of much of the scientific work with children under five. Important elements of work in science, such as observation, investigation and enquiry, pattern seeking, inference drawing and accurate communication, are evident in the best circumstances. Effective and interesting scientific activities enable children to observe carefully, to discuss what they see and, where appropriate, to record their observations (29).

observed. Subsequently the children drew the insects from direct observation. Most then went on to draw themselves.

47 Young children are fascinated by living things and natural phenomena and teachers use the many materials commonly found in and around nurseries and infant classrooms for pursuing children's interest in an increasingly scientific manner (30).

30

Much of this activity is planned to develop the children's awareness of similarities and differences and encourages careful observation and classification. Consideration of materials and their characteristics, or of various changes of state resulting from mixing and cooking ingredients when preparing food, for example, often leads to discussion. This is sometimes extended by considering the suitability of materials for particular jobs, as well as recognising things by their observable characteristics, including smell, feel, sound or taste. The following example shows how the children were able to experiment, discuss, observe carefully, predict outcomes and later to test their hypotheses.

29

A nursery class in the south

The sand tray had been filled with leaf litter for the day. On adjoining tables were large spoons, lenses, mirrors, drawing paper and a variety of pencils.

Four children started to investigate the leaf litter with their teacher. She spooned an insect into a viewer and passed it round for the children to look at. The children were absorbed in this activity for almost an hour during which they became adept at handling the insects and made interesting comments about them. Towards the end of this time the teacher gave the children a mirror so that they could look at themselves and compare their features with those of the creatures they had

A nursery school situated in the home counties

As a development of making biscuits the children in their final term were given containers each of which held a substance to be identified by smell, touch and taste. They each described what the substances smelled and felt like, making comments such as 'It feels like soft cement'. The substances were

*It may be useful to refer to the documents *Science 5–16: A Statement of Policy* and *National Curriculum Science for Ages 5–16*, DES, August 1988.

coffee, brown sugar, white sugar, cardamom and cumin powder, salt, chocolate milkshake powder, icing sugar and cornflour. They compared taste and commented that although some looked the same, for example, cornflour and icing sugar, they tasted differently. After some discussion about powders and crystals the children were asked to decide whether each substance was a powder or a crystal.

The children added water to their containers and were asked to predict what would happen when they stirred it. They observed the results and the teacher asked, 'Is the powder still there?' The word 'dissolved' was introduced: 'We cannot see it but we can taste it, where has the substance gone?' The children saw that the cardamom and cumin did not dissolve. They were then asked if it would be possible to get the sugar and salt back again from the water and the children thought not.

Stronger solutions of each substance were made and were left to see if the powders and crystals could be recovered later.

48 Early work in science also includes a consideration of living things and their interaction with the environment; energy, forces and their effects; and different natural materials in the classroom, for example wet and dry sand.

A first school in the south of England

Two sand trays had been provided, one containing wet and the other dry sand. Each tray had an identical range of carefully selected equipment: funnels, buckets, small plastic moulds and a sand wheel. Five four-year-olds were working side by side, three at the wet sand, two at the dry. Initially, and not untypically, those at the wet sand made castles but ignored the sand wheel, while in the dry sand all activity focused around pouring sand through the funnel and on to the wheel. The activities were observed by the teacher, who after some time intervened to make the activity more complex and to introduce elements of directed enquiry. Children using the dry sand and the sand wheel discussed their activities:

Child 1: 'It went round very fast.'
Child 2: 'A big lot of sand made it fast.'
Teacher: 'What happens when you have a little bit of sand?'

The child tipped a small amount of sand into the top of the funnel and watched.

Child 1: 'It's slow.'
Teacher: 'That's interesting, I wonder why that happened?'

The teacher left the children to experiment further and turned her attention to the wet sand tray and to the unused sand wheel.

Teacher: 'Have you used this?' (pointing to the sand wheel)
Child 2: 'It won't go.'
Teacher: 'Oh dear, I wonder why it won't go? Neesha, show them how you made your wheel go round.'

Neesha poured in a large amount of dry sand and the wheel rotated quickly.

Child 3: 'Our sand won't go.'
Teacher: 'Why won't your sand go?'

Teacher: 'Let's feel the sand, what does it feel like?'
Child 1: 'Cold.'
Child 2: 'Wet.'
Child 3: 'Sticky.'
Teacher: 'Let's feel Neesha's sand. What does that feel like?'
Child 1: 'It tickles.'
Child 2: 'Warm.'
Teacher: 'Yes, it tickles your hand when it runs through your fingers. Does the wet sand run through your fingers?'
Child 3: 'No, it's sticky.'

The activity continued using the plastic moulds and buckets; the teacher drew on the children's experiences and observations to enable them to reach some conclusions about the different properties of wet and dry sand.

49 Scientific enquiry often focuses on animals, plants and a variety of artefacts. Using these materials the children are encouraged to make accurate observations and, from time to time, to record some of them in an appropriate manner such as painting, drawing or modelling (31). In addition, the teacher records the children's spoken observations in writing; some children write their own simple statements. Such work clearly places considerable demands on the teacher's ability to give a structure to the children's experience which promotes progressive learning and capitalises on their interests and curiosity.

31

50 When children under five work in a scientific way they begin to learn that materials have different properties; they also learn about adaptation and change. The development of such scientific thinking and ideas can aid children's technological learning.

51 It is easy to underestimate the part that new technology plays in children's experience. Many of them are familar with remote control televisions, microwave ovens, digital clocks, calculators, programmable videos and home computers.

setting for hospital play. One patient was having his pulse rate taken; this involved both the 'doctor' and 'nurse' monitoring the passing of one minute using timers and watches. One section of the hospital corner had been established as an office and equipped with two telephones of different type, push-button and dial. The children used these to make telephone calls and the adults were careful to ensure that as the children dialled their calls the number recognition was accurate. The additional provision of an ansafone control, a typewriter, notepads and pencils encouraged children to convey messages in both spoken and written form (33).

32

33

Their experience of an everyday activity such as shopping may have more to do with credit cards and automatic tills in the supermarket than notes and coins in the corner shop. Effective work takes account of the children's changing experiences and draws upon them to develop learning, as well as to help young children to understand some of the technical complexities of modern living (32).

An infant school in the south

The four-year-olds in the reception class were pursuing a theme: 'People who Care for Us'. Part of the classroom had been adapted to provide a stimulating and well resourced

52 Young children in some nurseries and primary classes use microcomputers and other electronic equipment. Used selectively and well they help to develop the children's physical co-ordination and control while aiding their understanding of the technology and its applications.

A nursery class in a primary school in a London borough

The children had access to a programmable electronic toy. Small groups of children used this equipment to develop their early mathematical skills. For example, they developed an understanding of directional terms such as 'turn', 'forwards', 'backwards', 'left' and 'right'. They estimated how many of their strides would match the distance the toy vehicle had travelled and read and used number symbols to record what they had discovered. These children were developing skills in the use of technological equipment, learning spatial language, and at the same time developing an understanding of number.

53 Good provision for play and exploratory activity offers children opportunities to design and make things, and to choose which materials are appropriate for particular purposes. The provision of materials with varying attributes, such as size, shape, colour, rigidity, plasticity, hardness or other properties, gives children the chance to cut, measure and fit different shapes and sizes together, for example, in constructional activities such as making models.

54 Designing and making models helps to extend scientific work on energy and forces, for example, by making simple electric circuits using low voltage batteries; by considering the functions of a spring; and by the use of elastic bands or inflated balloons as sources of energy to make the models work. In nursery and primary classes children under five often play with simple machines, such as pulleys, water-wheels and cranes, and with the help of adults discuss what such machines do and how they work. Some use the large, simple diagrams provided with some constructional kits to make models (34) and occasionally try to draw a plan of their work.

55 Activities which develop technological experience derive from a wide range of sources. Well planned exploratory play offers children the chance to identify their own problems and to use their skills and knowledge to solve them.

34

An infant school in a large northern city

A group of boys and girls were making model fire engines from materials which included cereal boxes, wooden wheels, rubber bands and dowelling. A small toy vehicle was available for comparison and the teacher and children considered the number and location of the wheels and the position of the axles. The children were encouraged to estimate the length of the axle for their own vehicle by putting the dowelling against the box with the wheels roughly in place. The teacher marked where it had to be cut and each child in turn cut an axle using a small hacksaw and a simple safety device that prevented the wood from slipping. Questions from the teacher such as 'How long will the other axle need to be?' and 'How will you measure it?' prompted the children to use the first axle as a guide. One child marked off the place to cut as he had seen his teacher do earlier.

With some help from the teacher the axles were put in place and the children threaded on the wheels but found they fell off in use. They selected some rubber bands and wrapped them several times round the outer edges of the axle. They were then faced with the problem of the wheels being too close to the body of the vehicle and not running freely enough so the teacher asked what might be done. One girl said, 'We need a round thing to go there,' meaning a washer between the wheel and the body. Another child said, 'We can use another rubber band.' The teacher produced wooden beads with large holes and the first child used these as washers while the second child used rubber bands. The teacher asked them to try out their vehicles to see which moved more smoothly.

56 During the time that the children worked at this activity their skills and confidence developed. After each occasion when the teacher had given some specific help, for example by marking the wood and making holes in the body of the vehicle, the children took over these operations themselves. They had planned the design of their vehicle by discussing with the teacher that of the toy vehicle, decided on the materials to be used, estimated and measured them, solved some problems and tested and modified their design. Such work involves both boys and girls from an early age and effectively promotes positive attitudes and skills in science and technology.

AESTHETIC, CREATIVE AND PHYSICAL LEARNING AND EXPERIENCE

57 The development of aesthetic, creative and physical learning forms an integral part of much of the work already described. Good early-years education allows children to explore and experiment with two- and three-dimensional materials (35), to be creative and imaginative, to develop

35

their ability to handle tools, to use a range of techniques and to observe carefully. Such work is generally regarded as central to young children's learning and provides a wide range of valuable early experiences in music, drama, poetry and art, as well as extending physical development.

58 Many young children have daily opportunities to paint (36). In the

most successful schools they paint freely, mix the colours they need and represent what they see in their individual ways (37). In such cases the teachers encourage and guide the

37

children's efforts, helping them to become more competent. The most interesting work is often based on immediate events and social contacts and aspects of their personal development. Interesting events at home and school feature frequently in such work. Young children also enjoy painting patterns; some of the more mature ones successfully incorporate pattern into the pictures they paint. In some classes the under-fives use pencils skilfully to draw detailed pictures of people, natural objects, living things and artefacts, often showing good observation (38). Such activities also help children to develop the co-ordination and manipulative skills they need in learning to write.

36

38

59 Themes and centres of interest also provide many opportunities for children to use materials and equipment in creative ways and to use and extend the skills they have learned in earlier exploratory work.

A nursery unit in a small primary school in London

The focus of the work was 'colour' and in each of the three areas of the nursery displays were related to a particular colour. As part of the work based on 'yellow', a group of four children were drawing and painting a daffodil. Together with the teacher they looked at the flower and named the different parts. The teacher's questions helped to guide and develop the children's observations: 'What shape is the stem? Is it straight? What happens to it at the top near the flower? How do the petals join the stem?'

The children then started to describe the colour. One child said the flower was yellow and again the teacher's questioning led them to look more carefully.

Teacher:	'Is it all the same yellow?'
Child:	'No, the trumpet is dark yellow.'
Child:	'Some of the petals have got dark bits on the end.'

The teacher provided a range of paint brushes, powder paints, mixing dishes and paper. The children selected their own brushes and mixed their paint trying to match the colour of the daffodil. They were encouraged to experiment by testing out their colour on the spare paper until they were satisfied that they had mixed the correct colour.

60 Children under five develop musical skills very rapidly, sometimes by listening and responding to natural and man-made sounds and music. They create sounds and patterns with their voices, with simple home-made devices, or with good quality tuned and untuned instruments (39), all of which catch and sustain children's interest and result in work of quality.

3

A nursery school in London

The children were celebrating aspects of the Chinese New Year. They had listened to recorded Chinese music and had given considerable time to talking about the instruments and the thoughts and feelings which they inspired; in addition they had examined artefacts provided by the teacher. The teacher then hung a collection of metal items on a rack (spoon, ladle, mug, cake tin). A four-year-old picked up a drumstick and tapped each of the suspended items. Then he sang a song while accompanying himself on the metal objects. Subsequently he picked up the second drumstick and gradually created a sequence of sounds. This was sustained for some ten minutes when he introduced stamping into his sequence of sounds. After practising further he went to find the teacher so that he could perform his 'Chinese' music for her. She praised his performance and listened as he explained the whole process before presenting his musical composition to the group.

61 Young children enjoy singing rhymes and songs and rapidly develop a repertoire that they know by heart and sing as they play. They also listen to music and use the knowledge they gain to inform their own music-making. Teachers often plan musical activities which encourage children to work co-operatively and to refine the skills of the group.

A nursery school in the north-east

Music-making was based on direct experience and good provision which included a collection of relevant books and a variety of tuned and home-made percussion instruments, for example, shakers, xylophones made from dowel rods and chime bars made from angle brackets. A small group of children worked with the teacher, talking about the instruments and how they might be used in a simple ensemble. The children experimented with the instruments and suggested ideas which they tested. They demonstrated a high level of competence both in control and performance. They listened to each other critically yet supportively. They were not satisfied with impromptu or extempore playing and decided that their activity needed a framework. It was agreed that hand signals would be sufficient to denote starting and finishing times. It was clear that the children had such sessions regularly and that their level of competence was related to a carefully planned and progressive musical experience where the content and pace matched their needs.

62   An important element in the physical learning and experience of children under five is the development of their ability to use a range of tools correctly and safely. This is successfully achieved when teachers plan educational play that is well resourced.

A nursery class in the north

An area had been set up as a workshop which contained a wide range of appliances such as an iron, music centre, reel-to-reel tape recorder and radio set, as well as calculators, telephones and headphones. A tool box containing sand paper, pliers, screwdrivers, spanners and a drill was also available. Adjacent to the workshop was a woodwork bench and tools together with a collection of wood of different shapes, sizes and thicknesses and an assortment of nails of different lengths and gauges.

The workshop was used in a variety of ways to develop physical, exploratory, investigational and observational skills as well as for comparison and classification within the context of imaginative play.

A group of children used screwdrivers, pliers and sandpaper to 'mend' some of the equipment. One child noted the faults he had identified on a notepad. A second child sandpapered a wooden surface and screwed in imaginary screws. The two children discussed the action of the sandpaper, remarking that the paint was coming off and disappearing. When asked by the adult why they thought this was happening they replied that it was because the sandpaper had got sand stuck on to it and was rough. They then focused their attention on a reel-to-reel tape recorder and decided that they would 'repair' it. Using the tools they examined it most carefully and stated that when they pushed the switch down the power was on and when they pulled the switch up the power was off.

63   When such classroom skills are exercised by the adult, both planned and impromptu physical and creative play provide opportunities for young children to explore several areas of learning and experience simultaneously. As a result the children display an increasing competence and familiarity in handling materials.

64   Alongside these physical skills children develop strength as well as body and spatial awareness through movement in a variety of settings, both indoors and out (40, 41). Children under five are encouraged to run, jump, skip, climb and balance using a range of large climbing equipment, as well as

40

41

smaller apparatus, and to engage in physical activity in their educational play (42).

An infant school in London

As part of the work relating to the local environment the four-year-old children had been watching the building of a new super-market on a site opposite the school. This led to discussion about different types of buildings, with particular emphasis on the types of homes the children lived in.

In the outside play area was a collection of large wooden building bricks together with boxes and planks. A group of children started to build a house, discussing and modifying the design as they worked together. Eventu-ally, excited by their work, the children involved the teacher showing her the different parts of the house – the windows, how the door opened and closed and where the kitchen was. They decided that they would paint the house and the teacher asked them to estimate how many tins of paint they would need. They thought that six tins would be enough and filled six empty paint tins with water. The teacher provided them with decorators' paint brushes and rollers and they started to 'paint' the house. With the six tins of 'paint' they were able to cover the whole of the outside of the building. One child thought they should make a sign warning people about the wet paint and fetched a large sheet of art paper and a thick felt-tip pen. She 'wrote' the sign and read it to the teacher – 'be careful wet paint'. The teacher helped her to hang up the notice near the house.

42

65 In the best circumstances the work with under-fives in nursery schools and classes is well planned and progressive. It takes account of children's interests and appetite for play, building upon these to achieve educational objectives which complement, and have much in common with, the curriculum which they will receive in later years. This holds true for the work with four-year-olds in primary classes where the teachers have a sound understanding of the needs of this age group. However, in too many primary schools much of the work is not sufficiently differentiated to match the span of ability and range of needs in mixed-age classes which include four-year-olds.

66 Wherever the education of the under-fives takes place it should be informed by the essentials of good practice described earlier. It needs to take account of the different experiences which children have had prior to starting school, and be sufficiently differentiated to meet the needs of each child. The education that young children receive should not set up barriers to further achievement, nor should it be a hot-house forcing-ground. There is clear evidence that some children need much more practical activity and planned play than they now have in order to benefit from early education. Equally it is the case that some children have sufficient confidence, skills and understanding to be taken further than they are. The work described earlier shows how capable some of these children are, for example, the child who can handle numbers and see patterns so well that she is able to say 'I've got three threes, that's . . . 9' and later 'four threes, that's . . . 12'. Such children are already operating at level one of Key Stage 1 in the programmes of study for the National Curriculum.

67 This has important implications for the continuity between the teaching and learning of under-fives and that which takes place as children move into the statutory period of schooling. Clearly there is overlap between what children learn in these two phases. The teachers of under-fives need to know the curricular attainment targets and programmes of study for the first Key Stage 5 to 7, so that the experiences they provide for children take them towards, and in some cases cover, the early parts of the work. Equally infant teachers need to know what children have learned in the nursery and plan the work to take account of the stage the children have reached.

68 Given that parents will be informed of the progress expected of children within the levels and attainment targets of the National Curriculum, it is understandable that they will wish to see their children make a good start, particularly with aspects of reading, writing and mathematics. Parents will certainly not wish to see their children held back if they think them capable of tackling more challenging work than the teaching and provision for under-fives allows.

69 This is not to say that these elements have to be taught by methods which are widely agreed as unsuitable for young children. There is scope, however, for teachers to engage more effectively with the active learning patterns of young children in ways which promote the children's interest and competency in literacy and numeracy. An evident strength of successful teachers in these and other respects is their skill in teaching through well-timed discussion. The quality of the verbal interactions and clarity of the teacher's explanation in the best circumstances contrasts sharply with the lack of such well-judged teaching where the children are left too much to themselves. In the latter circumstances children's educational play may quickly degenerate into undemanding time-filling activities where the teacher's energies are spent coping more with the provision and organisation of materials than with teaching the children.

70 There are long-standing and considerable dilemmas for teachers serving in educational provision which caters for children from difficult social and economic backgrounds. The fact that much nursery provision for under-fives has been concentrated in certain urban areas acknowledges a set of special educational needs related to the children's disadvantaged social and economic circumstances. That such circumstances exist in other than urban settings is obvious. Nevertheless the greatest concentrations of social and economic difficulties faced by some schools are in urban areas where the teacher's task is made that much harder and complex than elsewhere.

71 In recent years there has been a great deal of debate about the value of education for the under-fives, how far it can be made to 'compensate' for social and economic disadvantage and whether it has lasting benefits.

72 The debate has also fuelled contention about how far the curriculum for the under-fives should differ from that, say, for older infants in emphasising certain aspects of children's development. At worst this has led to a polarisation of views in which, for example, sound objectives for children's social development have been set against equally valid objectives for their intellectual development.

73 Common sense suggests that the curriculum for the under-fives should reconcile these views and be just as balanced, broad and relevant to their particular needs as for older children. These principles are now established in law for pupils in maintained schools. In establishing a common curricular entitlement for all children the Education Reform Act has thrown into sharp relief issues of access to that entitlement and inevitably raised questions about the educational purposes and quality of provision for the under-fives. The best work with under-fives has always taken account of the need for continuity with the teaching and learning which takes place in the next stage of their education. The new legislation adds considerable importance to ensuring that full account is taken of the need to promote curricular continuity and progression.

Printed in the United Kingdom for HMSO
Dd 296757, C10, 12/93, 3396, 16268